Hogsheads to Blockheads

The Kids' Guide to Colonial Williamsburg's Historic Area

Barry Varela

Illustrations by Bentley Boyd

Colonial Williamsburg

The Colonial Williamsburg Foundation
Williamsburg, Virginia

20 19 18 17 16 15   3 4 5 6 7 8
Printed in China

Library of Congress Cataloging-in-Publication Data

Varela, Barry.
 Hogsheads to Blockheads : the Kids' Guide to Colonial Williamsburg's historic area/
Barry Varela ; illustrations by Bentley Boyd.
    p. cm.
 Includes index.
 ISBN 978-0-87935-245-5 (pbk. : alk. paper) 1. Williamsburg (Va.)--History--Juvenile
literature. 2. Williamsburg (Va.)--Guidebooks--Juvenile literature. 3. Colonial
Williamsburg (Williamsburg, Va.)--Guidebooks--Juvenile literature. I. Colonial
Williamsburg Foundation. II. Title.

 F234.W7V37 2010
 975.5'4252--dc22

                    2009053526

Designed by Helen M. Olds

Chowning's Tavern®, Christiana Campbell's Tavern®, Colonial Williamsburg®, King's Arms
Tavern®, Revolutionary City®, RevQuest: Save the Revolution!™, and Shields Tavern® are
marks of The Colonial Williamsburg Foundation, a not-for-profit educational institution.

The Colonial Williamsburg Foundation
PO Box 1776
Williamsburg, VA 23187-1776
colonialwilliamsburg.org/kids

Manufactured by Everbest Printing Co. Ltd., Guangdong, China
PO #367081 10/21/14 Cohort: Batch 1

Contents

Welcome to Williamsburg!

The first English settlers moved to the Williamsburg area in the 1630s, nearly four hundred years ago. In 1698, when the statehouse in nearby Jamestown burned down for the second time, the capital of the colony of Virginia was moved to Williamsburg. For most of the 1700s, Williamsburg was one of the most important cities in America. A number of famous heroes of the American Revolution, such as Thomas Jefferson and Patrick Henry, were regularly in and out of Williamsburg as elected members of the colonists' legislature (and Jefferson and Henry lived here as governors of Virginia after it became independent from England). However, in 1780 the Virginia capital was moved again, this time to Richmond, and Williamsburg lost its prominence. It became a sleepy, small town, known mainly as the home of the College of William and Mary.

Then, in the 1920s, the Reverend Dr. W. A. R. Goodwin, an Episcopalian minister at Bruton Parish Church in Williamsburg, became concerned that the town's old buildings were falling apart. He thought they should be saved, and he convinced John D. Rockefeller Jr., who was then the richest man in the world, to pay for the project.

Rockefeller bought up most of the oldest part of town, tore down buildings that had been built after 1790, and re-created the town as it had looked in the eighteenth century. Colonial Williamsburg's Historic Area was born. You can see public buildings like the Capitol, the Public Gaol, and the Courthouse. You can see the places where people lived, some rich and some poor, some free and some enslaved. You can see where and how people worked, making everything from wigs to wheels for horse-drawn carriages.

Although many buildings in the Historic Area were built in the eighteenth century and still stand today, some of the most prominent structures—the Governor's Palace, for example, and the Capitol—were destroyed by fire. They and several others are reconstructions based on architectural drawings, period illustrations, and other evidence. Eighty-eight of the buildings in the Historic Area are original. These include the Courthouse and the Magazine (where the colony stored its arms) and homes belonging to Revolutionary leaders like Peyton Randolph and George Wythe.

When you walk around Colonial Williamsburg's Historic Area, it's like traveling back in time. It's not just because of the buildings. You'll meet people who dress and talk and act as people did over two hundred years ago. Don't be shy. Ask questions.

There's no single best thing to see or do here. You may like the animals at Great Hopes Plantation best. You may think the guns stored in the entrance hall of the Governor's Palace are the coolest things in town. You may like stomping in the mud to help make bricks the way they did in colonial times. You may want to ride in a horse-drawn carriage or watch Colonial Williamsburg's young fifers and drummers march down Duke of Gloucester Street or imagine playing with the old-fashioned toys in the Abby Aldrich Rockefeller Folk Art Museum. You may want to rent some clothes and dress like the colonists did. If you're feeling brave, you may want to take a ghost tour at night.

There's also no single best way to use this book. You may want to read it from beginning to end. You may want to flip through it, reading only the parts that interest you, or you may want to take it with you as you explore Colonial Williamsburg's Historic Area.

Time Line

1630s The first English settlers move to the Williamsburg area.

1693 The College of William and Mary is founded in Williamsburg.

1698 The capital of Virginia is moved from Jamestown to Williamsburg.

1776 Virginia adopts its Declaration of Rights.

1776 The colonies declare their independence from Great Britain.

1780 The capital of Virginia is moved to Richmond.

1926 John D. Rockefeller and the Reverend W. A. R. Goodwin begin the restoration of Williamsburg.

Rare Breeds

Farm animals were much more a part of everyday life during colonial times than they are today. Oxen pulled wagons and carts through the streets and plows through the fields. Most people knew how to ride horses. Chickens, pigs, and cows were common backyard sights.

Over the last several centuries, breeding programs have created new strains of all these farm animals. Many of the breeds known to colonists have become almost unknown to modern farmers and ranchers. The Colonial Williamsburg Rare Breeds program works to preserve some of the descendants of these eighteenth-century farm animals and make them available for guests to see.

How rare is rare? A breed is considered rare if there are fewer than one thousand of the kind living in North America.

Colonial Williamsburg's Rare Breeds program includes the following farm animals.

Leicester Longwool Sheep

The Leicesters originated in eighteenth-century England and were prized for their long curly fleece, which was used to make wool, and as meat for the colonists.

American Milking Red Devon Cows

Colonists prized these cows both for meat and for their milk, which makes excellent butter and cheese.

American Cream Draft Horses

This is a rare modern breed that looks like some eighteenth-century draft horses used in the fields and also for pulling wagons and carts. You can recognize this horse by its cream-colored coat.

Canadian Horses

These horses are usually black or reddish brown with full manes and tails. Canadians are good riding horses. They are also good at pulling carriages and plows.

Milking Shorthorn Oxen, Randall Oxen, and Devon-Lineback Oxen

Oxen are cattle trained to pull heavy loads like wagons and plows. Clear out of the way if you see a team of oxen coming down the street!

Ossabaw Island Hogs

These hogs look very much like the hogs the colonists would have been raising for meat.

Poultry

Almost every colonial household raised chickens for food, that is, eggs and meat. In Colonial Williamsburg's Historic Area, you will find Nankin bantams, Dominiques, Red Dorkings, English game fowl, Silver-Spangled Hamburgs, and pigeons.

Not all animals that lived in colonial Williamsburg are rare breeds today. Just like today, in the eighteenth century people kept dogs and cats as pets. Sometimes pets had to work, however. Many cats were kept to kill rodents, and dogs helped to herd sheep, cattle, and pigs.

Wise to the Word

Leicester is pronounced "Lester."

Great Hopes Plantation

Even though Williamsburg was the focal point of Virginia in the 1700s, if you were growing up then, whether free or enslaved, you more likely lived on a farm like Great Hopes Plantation.

Colonials didn't have lightbulbs, but they did have oil lamps and candles.

Here you'll see log buildings like poor people and slaves lived in as well as simple frame structures. All the buildings were made with eighteenth-century-style tools and materials—starting from trees—just as it was done back then.

The buildings are surrounded by crops and pastures. You may see chickens scratching or pigs rooting around in the mud or powerful oxen helping to work the fields. Farming was hard work, but it was the most common way to make money in the eighteenth century, especially because everyone wanted tobacco. During the season, you can see tobacco growing in the field or curing in the tobacco house at Great Hopes. When it came to food, grains like corn and wheat ruled. Farmers also grew vegetables and raised livestock for meat and dairy products such as milk and butter.

Colonials didn't have canned or frozen foods, but they did have smoked and salted meats and pickled vegetables.

Great Hopes Plantation represents a typical eighteenth-century middle-class farm in this area, which is called Tidewater Virginia. The entire site from buildings to crops to livestock is based on the study of

twenty-five different planters who really lived back then. The work done here today is just like what they did.

Wise to the Word

A *middling* plantation like Great Hopes was owned by people who were neither very rich nor very poor. They often owned eight to fifteen slaves, but they also worked hard in the fields themselves.

Peyton Randolph House

Peyton Randolph was the president of the first and second Continental Congresses, which met in Philadelphia and were made up of delegates from the colonies. Randolph was one of the most important leaders in the time leading up to the American Revolution.

The Randolph house is actually two houses built in the early 1700s joined together with an addition. Just as interesting as the main house are the outbuildings that have been reconstructed on the property. These include a granary, two storehouses, a covered walkway, a large kitchen, a dairy, and a smokehouse.

Peyton Randolph owned twenty-seven slaves who lived and worked in the house and outbuildings. More than half of the people living in Williamsburg in the 1770s were African American, and most were enslaved. In some ways, the lives of the enslaved people who lived here were easier than the lives of those who worked on plantations. Cultivating tobacco, especially, was backbreaking labor. Slaves who lived in urban households like the Randolphs' usually had better clothes and food than those on farms, and they learned a lot more about what was going on in town. At the marketplace, slaves would exchange news and talk about friends and family. Sometimes, they could also help runaways.

Still, life in town was hard work and full of danger. Enslaved people in town often didn't get to live as families and didn't have as much privacy as those on farms. They lived over kitchens, laundries, and stables, and they often worked seven days a week.

At the Randolph house, even children under five years old had to learn how to act around the master. By the time they were five, they were put to work full-time doing chores like sweeping shells out of the grass and cleaning dishes and copper pots and pans. Cesar, Henry, and George, three boys between the ages of ten and fifteen in 1775, may have worked as stewards. They had to spend two to three hours each day serving a three-course meal to the Randolph family.

Wise to the Words

🥁 An *outbuilding* is a separate building from the house.

🥁 A *granary* is a storehouse for animal feed. The first syllable of the word can be pronounced with either a long or a short "a" sound.

Colonials didn't have flush toilets, but they did have outhouses and chamber pots.

Peyton Randolph

Peyton was the second of four children. His younger brother, John, has been called "John the Tory" because of his loyalty to the king.

Peyton served in the Virginia House of Burgesses, the first elected representatives of the people in a British colony in North America. Many colonists believed that the government in England should not be able to collect taxes from Virginians, especially since they had no representatives in Great Britain's Parliament. ("No taxation without representation!" was the colonists' cry.) In 1764, Peyton was at the head of a committee that prepared an address to the king protesting the Stamp Act. The Stamp Act, which went into effect in 1765, required colonists to pay a tax on almost all printed paper they bought, even playing cards. In 1766, the tax was repealed. Also in 1766, Peyton was elected Speaker (leader) of the Virginia House of Burgesses.

Despite the repeal of the stamp tax, tensions between the colonies and crown got worse, and in 1774 the royal governor of Virginia told the elected members of the House of Burgesses they could no longer meet. In response, Peyton and other former burgesses, along with leaders from the other American colonies, formed the first Continental Congress, which met in Philadelphia in September. Peyton was elected as its president.

At the second Continental Congress, in May 1775, Peyton was again elected president. Not too long after, in October of that year, while serving again in Philadelphia, he had a stroke and died. He didn't live to see the nation declare its independence on July 4, 1776.

The Original "Father of Your Country"

In 1775, after leading the second Continental Congress, Peyton Randolph was placed on the rebel execution list by the commander of British forces in America. When Peyton returned to Williamsburg, he was addressed by a company of men sworn to protect him with these words: "MAY HEAVEN GRANT YOU LONG TO LIVE THE FATHER OF YOUR COUNTRY, AND THE FRIEND TO FREEDOM AND HUMANITY!" Five months later, Peyton died of natural causes. It wasn't until years later that anyone thought to refer to George Washington as the father of his country.

Liberty for Me but Not for Thee

When the Revolution broke out, did slaves fight for the Continentals or the British? The answer is both.

Some slaves sided with the patriots, in support of the cause of liberty. More than five thousand blacks served in the Continental army and navy, and as a result many of them received their freedom after the war. Most white patriots, however, were interested in winning only their own freedom, not that of their slaves. The British promised slaves that, if they helped put down the rebellion, they would be given their freedom. Because the British lost the war, many of the former slaves who fought for them ended up back in slavery. Others were transported by the British to Canada, England, and the West Indies where they could be free.

Brickyard

Though most colonial buildings were made mainly of wood, people used brick for foundations, chimneys, and walkways. Grand buildings like churches and the Capitol were also made of brick so as to better resist fire. The Williamsburg Capitol building required about six hundred thousand bricks.

Rather than stay in a fixed location and ship bricks to where they were needed, the brickmaker would travel to the job site and create bricks there. Laborers, whether paid or slave, could always be found and trained on-site.

Colonial brickmaking consists of seven basic steps:

Clay and water are mixed together in the treading pit.

The clay mixture is shaped into a loaf, dusted with sand so it does not stick, and pressed into a mold. The excess clay is removed by drawing a straight, wooden stick across the top of the mold.

The filled mold is "off-beared," or carried to raised beds of sand for drying. The soft loaves are dropped out of the molds to dry in the sun. This job was often done by children.

After about a week, the unfired, or "green," bricks are moved to a drying shed, where they are protected from rain.

Once the brickmaker has the number of bricks he wants, all of the bricks are stacked up to make a giant kiln.

Wood is placed inside the fire tunnels of the kiln and set ablaze. The fire is kept burning, day and night, for about five days. QUICK TIP: If you're visiting in the fall, you may get to see the annual brick firing.

Two weeks after the fire is allowed to go out, the kiln is taken apart.

Fresh bricks ready for use!

Though brickmaking was considered unskilled labor, it wasn't easy. Brickmakers spent all summer in the hot Virginia sun, hauling countless loads of heavy clay and stacking up thousands of unfired bricks.

What's with All the Oyster Shells?

Colonial mortar—the white "glue" that goes between the bricks in a wall—was made of sand and lime. Colonists burned oyster shells and then soaked the burnt shells in water to produce lime. That's why you'll see piles of shells lying around the brickyard. Brickmakers, however, made only the bricks, not the mortar. The bricklayers—those who were doing the actual construction—made the mortar themselves.

Ooshy, Gooshy Fun

Want to get muddy? If you are here in the summer, here's your chance. Take off your shoes and take a stomp through the treading pit.

Wise to the Word

A *kiln* is an oven used to dry things like bricks or pottery. Some people pronounce the final "n" sound. Others pronounce the word as "kill." Either way is correct.

Colonials didn't have Play-Doh or Silly Putty, but they did have mud and clay.

Cooper

In the days before cardboard boxes and large metal containers, the easiest way to ship things was inside a wooden cask.

Casks could take a beating without falling apart or springing a leak. They were relatively light in spite of how much could be stored inside them. They came in many different sizes and could easily be stacked on a ship. Most importantly, they could be rolled, so even very large, heavy casks could be moved easily. Just about everything the colonists traded—wine, flour, boots, salt, fish, tobacco—was packed in casks for transport. Take notice of all the casks as you walk around town. They're everywhere!

It took many years of practice to become a master cooper, a person who makes casks and other wooden containers. Many large plantations had slaves working as coopers full-time. In the 1750s, Virginia coopers made about three hundred thousand casks yearly.

While visiting the cooper shed, stop a moment and inhale deeply. That's the odor of fresh-sawn wood—oak, hickory, and cedar. Smells good, doesn't it?

Wise to the Words

In colonial times, *cask* was the term for what we now call barrels. A *barrel* was a type of cask of a certain size. Other kinds of casks include the *butt*, the *pipe*, the *rundlet*, the *tierce*, and the *puncheon*. The different types of casks are different sizes. The most common type of cask was the *hogshead*, a container used to ship tobacco, the chief money-making crop in Virginia.

Hay's Cabinetmaking Shop

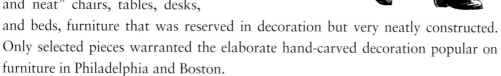

A cabinetmaker made more than just cabinets. Cabinetmaking included all kinds of fashionable wooden furniture. Williamsburg was one of Virginia's centers for furniture making. There was enough wealth in the prosperous colony to create demand for fine furniture. Virginians liked "plain and neat" chairs, tables, desks, and beds, furniture that was reserved in decoration but very neatly constructed. Only selected pieces warranted the elaborate hand-carved decoration popular on furniture in Philadelphia and Boston.

Black walnut, mahogany, cherry, poplar, yellow pine, oak, and beech were and still are used in Virginia cabinetmaking. Each wood has its own properties, which the master cabinetmaker has to understand. Some of the tools of the trade include saws, planes, drills, lathes, drawknives, and chisels.

Hay's Cabinetmaking Shop was run by a man named Anthony Hay until Edmund Dickinson rented the shop from Hay's widow in 1771. Dickinson later went on to captain a company of men under General Washington in the Revolutionary War. He was killed in battle in 1778.

A man who worked for Hay, Benjamin Bucktrout, later became an important furniture maker on his own and at one point rented Hay's shop. Bucktrout made a famous chair known as the Masonic Master's Chair. (The Masons were a semi-secret society to which many of the founding fathers, including George Washington, belonged.) Bucktrout advertised all sorts of services. He repaired musical instruments like spinets and harpsichords, sold wallpaper, repaired umbrellas, and, like most cabinetmakers, made coffins and provided other services for funerals.

Public Gaol

Built in 1704, the Public Gaol (jail) was mainly used to hold people who had been accused of crimes and were waiting to go to trial or who had been convicted of crimes and were waiting to be hanged.

At times, the Gaol also held debtors (people who owed money they couldn't pay back), runaway slaves, and the mentally ill. During the Revolution, Tories, spies, military prisoners, deserters, and traitors were imprisoned in the Gaol.

The Public Gaol wasn't like the prisons we have today, where inmates serve long sentences. In colonial times, either convicts were punished and let go or they were hanged. Sometimes a convicted felon was pardoned. There were few prison sentences.

The highest court in Virginia met only four times a year to try persons charged with serious crimes. If an accused person was convicted of a lesser crime, he or she

might be fined or the convict might be beaten at the whipping post. After receiving the punishment, the convict was set free.

If the crime was a felony and the sentence was death, the convict would be returned to the Public Gaol and held there until the hanging. A prisoner sentenced to death could be branded on the hand instead if he or she was shown mercy— T for theft, M for murder or manslaughter. The branding was painful, but then the prisoner got to go free. A second conviction usually resulted in a hanging.

Gaol inmates ate only one meal per day consisting of cornmeal and low-grade salt beef. They slept on loose straw and were lucky to have a blanket or two. Sometimes they were put in shackles. There were no fireplaces in the cells, so they were freezing cold in winter, and there was no air-conditioning in the summer. However, if they had enough money, inmates could buy what they wanted and have it brought to them in the Gaol. QUICK TIP: Be sure to check out the "throne," better known to you and me as the toilet!

Colonials didn't have toilet paper, but they did have leaves and corncobs.

The gaolkeeper and his family lived in a house attached to the Public Gaol. They had two rooms, a large hall and a bedchamber, on the first floor and another bedchamber on the second floor. Gaolkeepers were required by law to take prisoners to church on Sundays.

The gaolkeeper from 1771 to 1779 was Peter Pelham. Born in England, Pelham grew up in Boston, where he studied music. Around 1750, Pelham moved to Williamsburg. He worked as the Bruton Parish Church organist, and he taught harpsichord and spinet to young ladies. Pelham couldn't make enough money playing and teaching music to support his family, so he took the job at the Public Gaol. He and his wife, Ann, had fourteen children, though some died in infancy. At least five Pelham children grew up in the Gaol, and one was born there.

A number of prisoners escaped while Pelham was the gaolkeeper, leading some to believe that Pelham purposely allowed the prisoners to get away. An investigation cleared Pelham of all charges. Pelham wasn't the only gaolkeeper accused of allowing escapes. During colonial times, at least twenty-nine prisoners escaped from the Public Gaol!

QUICK TIP: Go into one of the cells and close the door behind you. Now imagine living in that small, dark room, all alone—or, worse, cooped up with some other wretched prisoner for weeks or months while waiting to be tried.

Wise to the Words

🛢 *Gaol* is pronounced "jail."

🛢 During the American Revolution, a *Tory* was an American who supported the British. Another name for a Tory was a *loyalist*.

🛢 *Shackles* are iron cuffs connected by a chain or bar that are locked around the ankles to prevent the prisoner from running.

Blackbeard's Crew

In 1718, the notorious pirate Edward Teach—better known as Blackbeard—was killed in a raid off the coast of North Carolina, paid for by the royal governor of Virginia. The fifteen or sixteen (historical accounts differ) surviving members of his crew were brought to Williamsburg and held in the Public Gaol before trial. All but two were convicted, sentenced to death, and hanged.

Blackbeard's first mate, Israel Hands, escaped hanging by agreeing to testify against his former shipmates. (Never trust a pirate!)

Samuel O'Dell, who may have suffered as many as seventy-five wounds during Blackbeard's last battle, told the court that he'd fallen in with Blackbeard's men to carouse and drink. He claimed he had no idea they were pirates. The judges must have believed him because they let him go. Either that or they felt sorry for him for having received all those wounds!

Colonials didn't have machine guns, but they did have rifles, muskets, and pistols.

The Revolutionary City

What would it have been like to live during the Revolution? Would you have been a patriot or a loyalist? If you had been enslaved, would you have run away to join the British? During Revolutionary City programming you become a part of these exciting—and dangerous—times.

Throughout the day, you can see all sorts of events and meet the men and women—rich and poor, great and humble, free and enslaved—who lived during the Revolution. You may run into an Indian trading with colonists or the traitor Benedict Arnold as he rides into town to convince the patriots to give up their fight. You can join other townspeople storming the Governor's Palace to demand the return of the gunpowder he took. You can even line up with the troops for inspection before they head off to Yorktown to win the war. Hear the debates, witness the fights, and join in the celebration of America's victory!

Fife and Drums

During the Revolution, some boys between the ages of ten and eighteen played an important role in the army. By playing fifes and drums, they relayed orders to soldiers in camp or on the battlefield and they provided a rhythm for marches. In the Revolutionary City, you can still hear the music and watch the marching of fifers and drummers.

Wise to the Word

A *fife* is a cylindrical instrument with six finger holes and a blowhole. Fifers blow across the blowhole rather than into it.

RevQuest: Save the Revolution!

Ever wanted to be a spy? RevQuest: Save the Revolution! is your chance. You will be assigned a top-secret task to help the patriots win the war. You may find yourself working to make France an ally against the British or to stop the assassination of a patriot leader. The success of the Revolution depends on you!

But undertaking these missions is not for the faint of heart. You will need to scour the streets for hidden clues and decode ciphers. Along the way, you will meet with other patriots who have information that will help you complete your assignment. Be careful not to trust anyone who doesn't know the code word—they may be the enemy.

Wise to the Word

A *cipher* is a code for transmitting secret messages. During the Revolution spies used many different ciphering techniques to try to keep their communications safe even if they fell into enemy hands.

Benjamin Powell House

Benjamin Powell was a successful carpenter who became an undertaker—not a funeral director, but what today we would call a *contractor*. He undertook the building and repairing of different kinds of public and private structures.

Among other projects, Powell repaired the Public Gaol, erected the steeple of Bruton Parish Church, and built the Public Hospital. Powell built his house around 1756. As one of the town's most skilled craftsmen, he built a fine home for himself and his family.

The mother of a well-to-do family like the Powells was in charge of mending clothes, cooking meals, cleaning the house, and supervising household slaves. Benjamin Powell's wife, Annabelle, also likely saw to the basic schooling of their two daughters, Hannah and Nancy.

Colonials didn't have elementary schools, middle schools, or high schools, but they did have schooling at home and colleges for wealthy boys.

Most well-to-do children learned to play musical instruments. Certain instruments were mainly for girls: the harpsichord, which is similar to a piano except that the strings are plucked rather than hammered; the spinet, a small harpsichord; and the guitar, a small stringed instrument similar to today's mandolin or lute. Other instruments were strictly for boys: the flute, the violin, the drum. Girls weren't allowed to play instruments that required their elbows to be held up away from their bodies. It wasn't considered ladylike for girls to assume such awkward postures.

Colonials didn't have CDs, DVDs, or MP3 players, but they did have harpsichords, violins, and other musical instruments.

In most households, the main meal of the day was dinner, served at about two o'clock in the afternoon. Supper was a late, light meal, often leftovers from dinner, served at about nine in the evening.

At the Benjamin Powell House, you can see young interpreters going about activities of daily life. Better yet, you can join in—dancing, playing, helping to cook, and having lessons just like those kids had in colonial times. The Powell House is not open year-round, so, if you want to go, make sure to check in advance.

Colonials didn't have rubber balls, but they did have balls made of inflated animal bladders.

Capitol

For most of the eighteenth century, Virginia's General Assembly met in the Capitol to write and administer the law. The General Assembly was called to order by the royal governor of Virginia. Most of Virginia's colonial governors, who were appointed by the king, lived in the Governor's Palace not far away. As the Revolution approached, the Governor's Palace came to symbolize the king while the Capitol symbolized the people of Virginia. The Capitol is also where the General Court sat to try both civil and criminal cases.

In 1699, the capital of Virginia was moved from Jamestown to Williamsburg. The first Williamsburg Capitol was completed in 1705, but it was gutted by fire in 1747. The second Williamsburg Capitol was completed in 1753. After the Revolution, the capital of Virginia moved to Richmond, where it still is today. The Capitol in Williamsburg was used as a law school and for various other purposes. The building burned down in 1823.

The building you see today was reconstructed in 1934. It is a replica of the 1705 Capitol.

Thomas Jefferson, Patrick Henry, George Washington, and other leaders of the American Revolution met and spoke at the Capitol. One of the most important events in American history took place here on May 15, 1776. That was the day Virginia's leaders declared their independence from England. They also told Richard Henry Lee to introduce a resolution for independence in Philadelphia, where leaders from all the British colonies in North America were meeting. That led, just a few weeks later, to the Declaration of Independence.

LOOK UP. What flag is flying on top of the Capitol? Is it the British flag, as it would have been before the Revolution? Or is it the Continental Colors, which was the American flag before the Continental Congress decided on the Stars and Stripes we're used to seeing?

Governor, Upper House, Lower House

The Virginia General Assembly consisted of the royal governor and two political groups: the upper house, or Council, and the lower house, or House of Burgesses. The Council consisted of twelve men appointed by the king on the recommendation of the royal governor. The House of Burgesses consisted of men elected by the people. Founded in 1619 at Jamestown, the House of Burgesses was the first elective body in British America. During the eighteenth century, the House of Burgesses consisted of two men from each county in Virginia. (Only white men who owned land, however, were allowed to vote.)

Seen from above, the Capitol is shaped like an "H." The governor and his Council used one side of the "H" and the House of Burgesses occupied the other.

Treason!

That's what some burgesses cried when Patrick Henry spoke at the Capitol to protest a law the British parliament passed called the Stamp Act. Many colonists agreed with Henry that the law was unfair to them, but others were loyal to England and thought Henry was a traitor. Henry's famous answer: "If this be treason, make the most of it!"

Two Declarations

One member of the House of Burgesses, George Mason, wrote that "All Men are by nature equally free and Independent" and that all had the rights to "the enjoyment of Life and liberty" and "pursuing and obtaining happiness." The burgesses agreed, and, on June 12, 1776, they passed Virginia's Declaration of Rights, which also said that people have the right to a trial by a jury and to freedom of the press and religion.

Does the Declaration of Rights sound familiar? That's because Thomas Jefferson used very similar words a month later when he wrote the Declaration of Independence.

Carpenter and Joiner

Carpenters work all over town, and joiners work in their shop just south of the Capitol. Theirs were good jobs to have because people could get all sorts of things from England but they couldn't import a house. Carpenters built and raised the shell of a house—its posts, beams, and frame. Joiners did the finer inside work like staircases, moldings, and window trims. Most carpentry is done on-site; most joinery is done in the shop.

Carpenters had to hoist up heavy timbers, and they had to be brave enough to climb up on a roof or out onto a beam. They also had to be good at drawing and math. A carpenter's apprentice had to work six or seven years before he earned his reward: cash, clothes, or—best of all—his own set of tools.

Carpenters work from the foundation of a building up to the roof. They lay floors, frame walls, raise rafters, hang doors, and lay shingles, among other things. Colonial carpenters sometimes used sandpaper to smooth out wood, but they often used other material, including rough reeds from a river or swamp or sometimes even sharkskin.

Charlton's Coffeehouse

In the eighteenth century, you didn't usually eat chocolate. Instead, you drank it, like our hot chocolate. (Chocolate didn't become a piece of candy until around 1850.) Chocolate, however, wasn't usually as sweet as we're used to today, and it was probably more of an adult drink, like coffee and tea. It was very popular and was served along with coffee and tea at eighteenth-century coffeehouses. You can see (and taste) for yourself at Charlton's Coffeehouse. The Coffeehouse is an exhibition site and not a working coffeehouse, but, as part of your tour, you can sample one of the colonists' favorite hot beverages: coffee, tea, or chocolate.

Then as now, people would gather at a coffeehouse to relax, read newspapers, and talk. Since this coffeehouse was so near the Capitol, the talk was often of politics.

In 1765, British Parliament passed the Stamp Act, which meant colonists had to pay a tax on almost all printed paper they bought, even playing cards. This tax probably annoyed a lot of people who liked to play cards at the Coffeehouse. In the fall of that year, an angry crowd cornered George Mercer, whose job was to sell the hated stamps. Fortunately for Mercer, the colony's royal governor, who was relaxing on the porch of the Coffeehouse, saw what was going on and took Mercer to safety. Mercer later resigned his job, and Parliament decided to get rid of the Stamp Act, but the incident near the Coffeehouse was a taste of the Revolution to come.

The Coffeehouse closed before the Revolution, and other buildings later took its place. To figure out what Charlton's Coffeehouse looked like and what went on there, historians and archaeologists pieced together all sorts of clues. For example, archaeologists found bones of a peacock. That led them to suspect that people at the Coffeehouse might have eaten the birds.

Opened in the early 1760s, the Coffeehouse was owned by Richard Charlton, a wigmaker. His customers included George Washington and Thomas Jefferson. Still, Charlton didn't make a lot of money from the coffeehouse, partly because times were hard after the French and Indian War and maybe also because people tended to sit a long time without buying much. By 1767, Charlton closed the coffeehouse.

Pasteur & Galt
Apothecary Shop

Eighteenth-century medicine was a combination of old and new: old treatments that went back to the ancient Greeks and Romans and new discoveries from the Renaissance and eighteenth-century science. There were various theories about how a body became ill and how to treat illness.

Children were often sick with some of the same illnesses we get today, including colds, earaches, measles, and chicken pox. Even though no one knew in the eighteenth century that bacteria and viruses made people sick, it was known that diseases spread from person to person. But, because they didn't understand that you didn't have to actually be sick to carry germs, sometimes apothecaries and midwives unknowingly carried disease from one patient's home to another.

Medicines were made from plants, minerals, chemicals, and animal products. While very few medicines cured diseases, they did help people feel better. As another type of treatment, the patient might be bled with leeches or by opening a vein. Then again, the patient might be given a drug to induce vomiting or diarrhea.

Apothecaries in the colonies didn't usually go to medical schools to study medicine. Like many tradespeople, most apothecaries learned their trade by serving as apprentices. This shop, however, features copies of Dr. Galt's certificates from St. Thomas's Hospital in London for training completed in surgery. He was also trained elsewhere in medical theory and midwifery.

Colonials didn't have antibiotics, but they did have leeches and herbs.

Just like our modern drugstores, the colonial apothecary made money by stocking items other than medicines. Coffee, candy, spices, soap, and toothbrushes were just a few of the many things you could find at the colonial apothecary.

Colonials didn't have Band-Aids, but they did have cotton dressings.

Take a look at the Pasteur & Galt Apothecary Shop sign. The mortar and pestle was a traditional symbol for this trade. It was used to grind and mix medicines. The staff with a snake wrapped around it refers to Aesculapius, an ancient god of medicine.

Modern Treatments Based on Old Remedies

Some of the treatments that colonial apothecaries used are still used today. Chalk was used for heartburn, coffee for migraines, and chocolate for coughs. Today, chalk is a common ingredient in heartburn medicines, and caffeine is often used in medicines for headaches. In the future, you may even see chocolate in cough medicines.

Wise to the Words

🏺 An *apothecary* is a pharmacist or druggist. The word can also refer to the shop of a pharmacist: a drugstore.

🏺 A *leech* is a worm that sucks blood.

🏺 A *midwife* is a woman trained to assist in childbirth. Dr. Galt, as well as other doctors in town, advertised himself as a "MAN-MIDWIFE."

Raleigh Tavern

In colonial times, if you were hungry, thirsty, tired, or just in need of some good company, a tavern was the place to go. At the Raleigh Tavern, you might bump into Peyton Randolph, George Washington, Patrick Henry, or Thomas Jefferson. On May 27, 1774, royal governor Lord Dunmore dissolved the House of Burgesses for objecting to the closing of the Port of Boston after the Boston Tea Party, and eighty-nine former burgesses reassembled at the Raleigh Tavern. The Raleigh Tavern was also where Williamsburg citizens gathered to celebrate when word came that the United States of America had won independence from Great Britain.

The original Raleigh Tavern burned down in 1859. The one you see today was built in 1932, based on plans of the original building. Written over the mantel in the Apollo Room, these Latin words appear once again: *Hilaritas Sapientiae et Bonae Vitae Proles*, which means "Jollity, the offspring of wisdom and good living."

Sign of the Times

The tavern sign has a picture of Sir Walter Raleigh, after whom the tavern is named. Raleigh was famous for having spread his best cloak over a puddle so Queen Elizabeth could walk over it. That story may just be a legend, but Elizabeth did like Raleigh enough to give him permission to colonize America. Raleigh organized the first English settlement in America at Roanoke Island off the coast of what is now North Carolina. The settlement is known as the Lost Colony since no one knows for sure what happened to the settlers.

Wise to the Words

 Nowadays, a *tavern* is a bar. In colonial times, taverns provided food, drink, a place to sleep, and a place for guests' horses. People went to taverns to dance, smoke, play cards and dice, and just spend time with their friends. Taverns sometimes rented space to political groups, scientific societies, and other organizations and clubs. Women did not usually stay overnight in a tavern.

🪘 Colonists drank beverages named *lamb's wool*, *stitch*, *kill devil*, *grog*, *flip*, *syllabub*, and *bumbo*.

Silversmith
(The Golden Ball)

During the eighteenth century, there were fifteen or sixteen silversmiths working in Williamsburg, though not all at the same time. One of them was James Craig, a British silversmith who opened a store in 1765. A few years later, he hired a watchmaker and named the store the Golden Ball.

Silversmiths hammer silver to form the material into the many items they make. Williamsburg silversmiths made mostly small objects like spoons, buttons, and buckles. Occasionally, a silversmith would make a larger piece, such as a mug or ladle. Silversmiths also did repair work.

The tradespeople who work in the Golden Ball today make beautiful silver jewelry, flatware, and hollowware by hand, just like Craig did over two hundred years ago. Their work, along with other silver and gold jewelry in the style of the eighteenth century, is for sale in the store next to the workshop. (You need an admission ticket for the workshop but not for the store.)

Wise to the Words

🪘 *Flatware* is eating and serving utensils and other relatively flat tableware like plates and saucers. *Hollowware* is tableware such as bowls and cups that have an unfilled space, or are hollow.

🪘 *Rottenstone*, also called *tripoli,* is powdered limestone used in polishing silver.

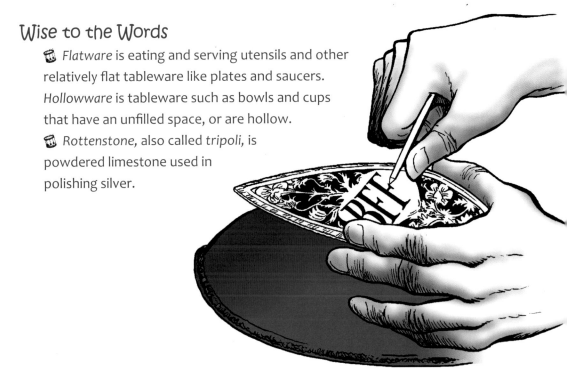

Milliner and Tailor
(Margaret Hunter Shop)

At the Margaret Hunter Shop today, interpreters portray the millinery and tailor businesses. In the eighteenth century, milliners were almost always female, and tailors were almost always male.

Millinery has come to mean "hat shop," but in colonial days milliners made and sold much more than hats. The milliner herself made various accessories for women, men, and children. If she owned a shop that sold things, she also stocked such items as shoes, needles and thread, ribbons, books, dolls, games, liquor, and hundreds of other items. QUICK TIP: If you see something behind the counter that interests you, don't be shy. Ask if it can be brought out for you to examine.

Although the Margaret Hunter Shop did not employ a mantua-maker in the eighteenth century, it was then common for milliners and mantua-makers to work together, as they do in the shop today. While milliners made accessories, such as shifts, mitts, and bonnets for women and shirts, handkerchiefs, and cravats for men, mantua-makers made gowns, better known to us as *dresses*.

When making women's gowns, mantua-makers didn't use patterns. They made gowns to fit their customers' stays. Stays are rigid undergarments that fit snugly from under the arms to the waist. If the stays fit the customer properly, then a gown made to fit the stays would fit the customer, too.

Today, the tailors share space with the milliners and mantua-makers. Tailors make clothing for men, women, and children, both rich and poor. They make clothing as diverse as gentlemen's fine suits, young boys' leather breeches, field slaves' jackets, ladies' riding habits, stays for women and children, and much more.

The word *tailor* means "one who cuts" in many languages, and it is the cut of the fabric that makes a garment fit the body. The master tailor's greatest skill is the precision required to measure the customer, draw patterns, and cut the cloth to make garments that fit exactly. Journeymen and apprentices stitch, press, trim, and finish the garments.

A Passion for Fashion

Just like today, men and women in colonial times were very interested in dressing in the latest fashions. Hat styles, skirt styles, petticoat styles, jacket styles all changed constantly—and sometimes very quickly.

People in Williamsburg learned about fashion from magazines and newspapers brought over from England. Of course, by the time the papers got to America, they were six or eight weeks old, but that didn't matter. A trend was a trend even if it was a little dated.

Milliners encouraged their customers to keep up with the latest fashions. They sold more clothes that way!

Colonials didn't have zippers or Velcro, but they did have buttons.

Two Williamsburg Milliners

Margaret Hunter was a real person. She was born in England. She had a sister, Jane, who was also in the millinery business. Margaret died in 1787. Beyond that, we don't know much about her.

Catharine Rathell was a milliner in Williamsburg who decided to return to England at the outbreak of the Revolution. She packed up her wares and took ship for her mother country. The ship ran aground on a sandbar about twenty miles from the Liverpool harbor. Catharine Rathell was thrown overboard and drowned just as she was nearly home.

Wise to the Words

🛢 In the eighteenth century, the word *dress* referred to the overall style of clothing. The word *gown* was used to refer to the woman's garment that we call a dress. *Mantua* was an earlier term for the word *gown*.

🛢 A *waistcoat,* pronounced "wescut," is a man's vest.

Post Office, Printing Office, and Bookbindery

In 1730, William Parks set up the first printing press in Williamsburg. A few years later, he was publishing the colony's first newspaper, the *Virginia Gazette*, printed weekly. Besides printing newspapers and books, Parks ran the post office and booksellers' shop, sold writing supplies, and did bookbinding.

Colonial printers didn't have computers to set type like modern-day printers do. They had to pick individual metal letters out of huge trays of type. Capital letters were in the upper case. Small letters were in the lower case. Sound familiar? We still call capital letters *uppercase* letters and small letters *lowercase*.

The bits of type were then set, by hand, one by one in rows to make up words and sentences. They were made in mirror image and set from right to left so that the printed page would read correctly, left to right. The lines of type were locked in a frame. A person called a *beater* used two ink balls to beat a layer of ink evenly onto the type. Ink balls were hollowed-out pieces of wood stuffed with wool and covered with leather. Each ink ball had a wooden handle for the beater to hold onto it. After the type was inked, a sheet of paper was pressed against it. To make another copy, ink was reapplied and a new sheet of paper pressed. Each impression took as little as fifteen seconds. It was

Colonials didn't have pens, but they did have feather quills and ink.

a slow process compared to our modern presses but a lot faster than writing with a quill pen.

Colonials didn't have television or radio, but they did have books, newspapers, and almanacs.

Bookbinders folded, pressed, sewed, and trimmed pages to make pamphlets and books. Some books were bound with calf, sheep, or goat leather. Did you notice those tools with the long handles and wheels that look like pizza cutters? Those are finishing wheels. Each tool has an engraved design that is used to decorate the leather of bound books. The finest books were also decorated with gold leaf on their covers. Books were very expensive, so very few people had many books.

At the Post Office, located above the Printing Office and Bookbindery, you can purchase some of the items made by today's printers and binders. You can mail a letter or postcard from the Post Office, and it will be canceled with a special postmark.

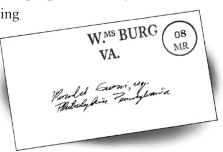

Virginia Gazettes

In 1775, Williamsburg had three newspapers competing with each other. All three had the same name—the *Virginia Gazette*!

Wise to the Word

🛢 Ink was made of varnish and lampblack. *Lampblack* is a finely powdered black soot.

James Anderson's Blacksmith Shop and Public Armoury

Think of all of the everyday things that are made of iron and steel: forks, knives, and spoons for serving and eating, rakes for cleaning the yard, nails for joining things, and hinges and knobs on doors and cabinets. In the eighteenth century, the blacksmith made all of these things by hand. Working in the hot blacksmith shop forging these tools out of iron and steel was hard work.

When the War for Independence began in 1775, the priorities of the blacksmith changed. What else is made of iron and steel parts besides tableware and door hinges? Guns, bayonets, and swords— the tools of soldiering. The blacksmiths in Williamsburg didn't make many guns, but they did repair them when they were damaged, and that was just as important.

Blacksmith Shop

Imagine a bar of steel that reaches from the floor to the ceiling, and then imagine that this same bar can be turned into just about anything,

from a musket to a kitchen spoon. The blacksmith and his apprentices heat these tall iron and steel rods and pound them into new shapes. When heated in the coals, the iron turns red, orange, and finally yellow. When it is hot enough, it can be as soft as clay. The blacksmith then holds it with tongs and uses a hammer to flatten and shape it.

James Anderson was the most successful blacksmith in Williamsburg. He did work for the citizens of the town and for the government. During the War for Independence, as public armorer, Anderson repaired muskets, swords, bayonets, and other weapons for Virginia. Among the workmen in the shop were young apprentices, older journeymen, American soldiers, French soldiers, enslaved Africans, and British prisoners. It was a very busy site!

Colonials didn't have air conditioning, but they did have open windows.

It's Hot Here!

In addition to his other tools, a blacksmith needs a forge to heat the metal. A bellows is used to blow air into the fire to increase the heat. Iron begins to soften when it is red hot (about 1,000°F) and will melt when it reaches white hot (about 2,700°F). When the fire is being fanned, it burns at about 3,000°F. The smith has to judge the temperature by its color. As long as the metal is glowing, it is soft enough to work with the hammer. Swinging a hammer all day around the fire is hard, tiring work, especially in the heat of summer.

Tin Man

Even though guns are one of the most important tools in a war, they weren't the only things that soldiers needed. One thing that they needed every single day was food. Transporting food was important because soldiers were often on the move. The best part about the tin cans and kettles made by the tin man—other than the fact that they were often filled with food—was their weight. While containers made of iron would have been incredibly heavy and difficult for the soldiers to carry with the rest of their supplies, tin is so light that soldiers could pick it up with just one finger. When you visit the tin shop, ask the tin man to let you hold one and see for yourself.

Wigmaker
(King's Arms Barber Shop)

At the colonial barber shop, a man could get a haircut and a shave. That's not surprising. What may be surprising is that some colonial barber shops also sold perukes, or wigs.

Wigs have been around since antiquity. The Greeks, the Romans, and the Egyptians all wore wigs. Upper-class Europeans started wearing perukes in the early 1600s. Over time, perukes became larger and more elaborate until by 1700 the fashionable gentleman was balancing on his head an enormous mass of cascading curls. Over the next one hundred years, perukes, or periwigs as they came to be known, shrank in size until they became the modest wigs you see people in Williamsburg wearing.

Wigs might be made of horse, goat, yak, or human hair. White hair powder consisting of wheat or bean flour was applied to perukes to give them a more formal air. A cone-shaped mask was used to protect the face from the powder when a person already had the wig on. Pomades (scented oils) were used to secure hair powders to the wig or to the hair of a customer. An inexpensive wig could be made in less than a week whereas a "big wig" could take as many as three weeks or more.

Ladies as well as men wore wigs. Keep in mind, in order to wear a custom wig, the head had to be kept shaved. Yes, that applied to ladies, too.

Well-to-do men and ladies owned several wigs in a variety of styles and colors for different occasions. There were casual wigs for daily wear and formal wigs for special events.

Popular wig colors included black, brown, white, grizzle (meaning gray), blond, and chestnut. Red was an unfashionable hair color and was rarely seen.

In addition to wigs, the wigmaker sold ladies' curls, knots, and braids and men's queues and side curls.

Bloody Barbering

For hundreds of years, during the Middle Ages and the Renaissance, barbers were doctors and dentists as well as haircutters. In fact, they were called *barber surgeons*. Barber surgeons pulled teeth, removed tonsils, and performed other surgeries. They also practiced bloodletting, the cutting open of a person's vein, which was believed to be a cure for many ailments. In the 1740s, the profession of barber surgeon was split into the two professions of barbers and surgeons. *Barbers* were not allowed to do surgery, and *surgeons* were not allowed to do barbering.

Hair Today, Gone Tomorrow

In 1763, a group of English peruke-makers wrote to the king complaining of men who preferred to wear their own hair: "This mode, pernicious enough in itself to [our] trade, is rendered excessively more so by swarms of French hairdressers already in [London and Westminster], and daily increasing." Despite this complaint, wigs continued to be fashionable throughout the American Revolution. The French Revolution was the beginning of the end for wigs. (The French Revolution started in 1789 in case you are wondering.)

Wise to the Words

The word *peruke* comes from the French word *perruque*, meaning "wig." Over time, *peruke* came to be pronounced "perwick," then "periwick," and finally "periwig." The word *wig* is just a shortening of *periwig*.

🎨 *Queues* is pronounced "kews." Queues are false braids added to the man's own head of hair.

🎨 A *blockhead* is a solid piece of elm or ash carved to the size and shape of a customer's head. Wigs were built on blockheads to ensure a perfect fit. Even in the eighteenth century, this word for a wooden head—a head with no intelligence in it—was also used as an insult.

🎨 The *powder room* was a small room where ladies and gentlemen could go to have a little privacy to "powder" their wigs.

James Geddy House

Built in 1762, the James Geddy House was the site of James Geddy's silversmith business and where he lived with his wife and children. Much of the original house still remains.

Born in 1731, James Geddy was the most successful silversmith in Williamsburg. He made enough money from his business to buy farmland, nearly placing him in the same class as the rich land-owning gentry who governed Virginia. James Geddy moved to Petersburg, Virginia, in 1778 and died in 1807.

Sometimes you can see young interpreters at the Geddy House doing things the Geddy children did, such as practicing letters on slates, reading eighteenth-century books, sewing, or playing board games or cards. Outside they—and you—might play with rolling hoops or ninepins (a game like bowling).

For Sale

Between 1766 and 1777, Geddy advertised the following as available for sale in his silversmith shop: silver, gold, and diamond rings; earrings, brooches, necklaces, and lockets; shoe buckles, knee buckles, and neck buckles; gold, silver, and crystal buttons; silver watches, watch keys, and watch chains; silver teaspoons, ladles, and cream buckets; tortoiseshell combs; silversmith, goldsmith, and watchmaker tools; and thimbles, pins, bells, pocketbooks, and many other items.

Gunsmith and Foundry

Behind the James Geddy House is the Gunsmith and Foundry, where James Geddy's brothers, David and William, plied their trades. Founders work with molten pewter, lead, brass, and bronze to make bells, shoe buckles, sword hilts, and many other items.

Colonial founders used the sand cast method, which involves pouring molten metal into molds made of a mixture of sand and clay. Be sure to ask the founders to explain the process to you. Check out the huge bellows, which blows air through the furnace and raises the temperature of the fire.

Gunsmithing was one of the most demanding trades of the colonial period. It requires many of the same skills as a blacksmith, a whitesmith, a founder, a woodworker, and an engraver—all wrapped up in one.

Since the colonists imported most of their guns from England, most of what the colonial gunsmiths did was repair work. In England, the making of guns had become specialized. There were craftsmen who made nothing but flintlocks. Others made nothing but barrels. Others worked only on the wooden stocks. This division of labor was the beginning of interchangeable parts and assembly-line production—the roots of the Industrial Revolution and the factory system that replaced the handmade culture of the eighteenth century.

Lock, Stock, and Barrel

The three main parts of a gun are the *lock* (the firing mechanism), the *stock* (the wooden part that held the lock and barrel in place), and the *barrel* (the long metal tube).

Fired Up, Ready to Go

Most colonial firearms made use of a firing mechanism called the *flintlock*. Flint is a kind of stone that, when struck with steel, sends out a hot spark. In a flintlock gun, a piece of flint is set in a spring-loaded cock that can be pulled back and latched in place, or cocked. When the trigger is pulled, the cock is released, driving the flint into a steel face and creating a spark. The spark lights a small gunpowder charge in an external pan. That powder explodes, sending a flame through a small hole in the barrel and lighting the main gunpowder charge inside the barrel. When the main charge explodes, the ammunition (whether ball or pellets) is shot at great speed through the barrel toward the target.

Wise to the Words

A *foundry* is a workshop where metal is melted in a furnace and poured into molds.

Pewter is a mixture of metals, mostly tin with a little copper and antimony (a metallic element).

A *whitesmith* is a tradesman who works with "white," or light-colored, metals such as tin and pewter. The word also applies to metalworkers who file or polish iron bright, or white.

A *rifle* is a long gun with several spiraled grooves in the barrel to put a spin on the ball or bullet. A *musket* is a military long gun with an ungrooved barrel. A spinning object moves through the air in a straighter line than does an object that isn't spinning, so rifles are more accurate than muskets.

Colonials didn't have dynamite, but they did have black gunpowder.

BANG!

Colonial Garden and Nursery

The Colonial Garden and Nursery features historically accurate plants and gardening tools. Take a look at the rakes and wheelbarrows, for example, and see how they differ from what people use today. Look for the thumb pots for watering plants. Think about how often you would need to refill the pot to water a whole garden! Ask the gardeners if they need help. You might get a chance to help with the planting, watering, or weeding if you are there at the right time.

Many famous Virginians loved to garden. John Randolph, attorney general of the colony of Virginia at the beginning of the Revolution, wrote a pamphlet on gardening in Virginia. His cousin Thomas Jefferson cultivated his own gardens at Monticello.

From March through December, the garden's shop is open, and you can buy plants, seeds, tools, and other garden items like those used in the eighteenth century.

Weaver

A weaver, with spinning wheel, looms, dyes, yarns, and cloths, works on Duke of Gloucester Street.

Up until the Revolutionary period, the vast majority of cloth used by Virginians was imported from England. When war broke out, Americans had to start producing their own cloth.

Williamsburg weavers made cloth from wool, cotton, flax (linen), and hemp. Not unlike weavers of two hundred years ago, today's weaver gets his wool from a pasture just down the street. As part of its Rare Breeds program, Colonial Williamsburg raises Leicester longwools, a rare breed of sheep. Sometimes you can see the sheep right behind the weaver's shop.

Dyes were made from spices, nuts, roots, tree barks, and insects. Red dye, for example, was made from a South American bug called the *cochineal*. These bugs were readily available in Virginia until the Revolution. It took about seventy thousand of them to make a pound of red dye. The dye was used for coloring not only fabrics but also paint, foods, and ladies' lips and cheeks. When it was used as makeup, it was sometimes mixed with rice powder, but not always: sometimes ladies applied just the crushed bugs directly to their skin.

Shoemaker's Shop

It took several workers to produce shoes, dividing up the tasks between them. In one work week (six days), four men could make twenty-four pairs. It was a popular trade. Everyone needs shoes, shoes constantly wear out, and the work was more pleasant than many other trades.

Shoes are made on lasts, foot-shaped wooden forms. In the eighteenth century, most shoes were made on a *straight last*, meaning the last did not provide any curve to the shoe. When a shoemaker uses a straight last, there are no left and right shoes: both shoes in a pair are made on the same last. This procedure cuts in half the number of lasts that a shoemaker has to have on hand. You might be surprised to learn that a pair of shoes made on a straight last is not necessarily less comfortable than a pair of shoes made on left and right lasts.

George Wilson's was one of twelve or more shoemaking businesses operating in Williamsburg in the 1770s. Besides local shops, there were several large shoe-making firms in nearby cities. One of these employed thirty men. Shoes were also imported from England.

In a 1773 advertisement, Wilson offered "a choice Cargo of the best Sorts of ENGLISH LEATHER for all Manner of Mens Shoes and Pumps, and excellent LONDON DRAWLEGS for BOOTS." Imagine being able to pick out the piece of leather your shoes would be made from!

Wise to the Words

🪘 *Shoemakers* create shoes and boots. *Cobblers* repair them.

🪘 Shoemakers have some unusual names for their materials and tools. The *vamp* is the piece of leather that covers the toes in the shoe's upper. The *quarters* cover the heel, so there are four of these pieces in one pair of shoes, hence the name. A *helling stick* was a piece of wood used to polish the edges of the sole. A *petty boy* was a tool to polish soles and heels. The shoemaker's tool kit was called *St. Hugh's bones.* According to legend, St. Hugh worked as a shoemaker. After he died, his friends made his bones into shoemaking tools.

Courthouse

Near the center of Duke of Gloucester Street, you'll find the Courthouse, a large brick building with a six-sided cupola on top. Built between 1770 and 1771, the Courthouse was the meeting place of the hustings court and the James City County Court. The hustings court dealt with crimes committed within the city limits and also handled estates, deeds, wills, and other civil matters. The James City County Court dealt with crimes committed outside the city.

People accused of committing minor offenses, such as failing to go to church or small thefts, were tried at the Courthouse. Free citizens accused of more serious crimes were tried at the Capitol in the General Court. Enslaved people were tried at the Courthouse regardless of the seriousness of the crime.

The Courthouse was often packed with spectators hoping to be thrilled by tales of temptation unresisted. Convicts would be punished immediately. They might be flogged at the whipping post and sent home, or they might be placed for hours in the pillory or the stocks, where their fellow citizens could make fun of them.

The mayor and the city council met in the Courthouse. It was also where important announcements were made and documents posted. In 1776, the Declaration of Independence was read aloud from the Courthouse steps.

Wise to the Words

🥁 A *cupola* is a small domed structure that rises from the top of a roof or larger dome.

🥁 A *pillory* is a heavy wooden frame with holes for the hands and head. Offenders were locked in a pillory and exposed to public scorn. *Stocks* are a wooden frame in which holes have been cut out so that the feet or the feet and hands of the offender could be locked. QUICK TIP: You can try out the stocks and the pillory and even get your picture taken in them if you want. Smile!

Market House and Market Square

The newest building to go up in the Historic Area is the Market House. It made sense to build the Market House in the center of town in the 1750s (and to build it here again in 2015) because this is where everyone came to buy and sell vegetables, fruit, meats, fish, eggs, and other produce. In those days there were no refrigerators, so if you wanted to eat fresh food, you had to buy it every few days. All sorts of people—men and women, boys and girls, free and enslaved—went to the Market House.

Colonials didn't have supermarkets, but they did have outdoor markets.

Kids had important jobs at the Market House. Kids from the country would help load up wagons and sell the foodstuffs, and kids from town would help carry the purchases. There were fun things to buy, too (then and now), such as hats and toys and games. "Baker boys" would sometimes get into trouble if they were caught racing the wheelbarrows loaded with bread for the Market House.

Around the Market House is Market Square. On two days of the year, April 23 and December 12, Market Square hosted the official town fair. The fair was like a huge party with dancing, games, horse races, cockfights (with roosters), beauty pageants, and puppet shows.

Colonials didn't have shopping carts, but they did have baskets.

Market Square is also where the colonial militia would assemble. Most able-bodied free men between the ages of sixteen and sixty belonged to the militia. The whole town would come out to watch the militia train and drill.

Magazine and Guardhouse

Across from the Courthouse, on Duke of Gloucester Street, is the Magazine, an unusual eight-sided brick building, and the Guardhouse.

At times, the Magazine contained up to three thousand muskets and sixty thousand pounds of gunpowder. Swords, tents, cooking utensils, and other tools of warfare were stored there as well. Because the Magazine held so much valuable and dangerous material, during the Seven Years' War, also called the French and Indian War, a high wall was built around it and the Guardhouse was constructed nearby.

The Gunpowder Incident

By the spring of 1775, talk of revolution was spreading. Fearing that colonial militias were planning to rebel, the king ordered Virginia's and other colonies' royal governors to take the colonies' gunpowder stores and hide them. On April 20, Virginia's royal governor, Lord Dunmore, ordered the gunpowder removed from the Magazine and placed on a ship in the James River. This was done in secret, in the middle of the night.

When the citizens of Williamsburg discovered the plot, they were outraged. They had paid for the gunpowder and believed the royal governor had no right to take it from them. About ten days later, word reached Virginia of shots fired at Lexington and Concord between the redcoats and the Massachusetts militia. War had not yet been declared, but the battle in Massachusetts and the stolen gunpowder did not sit well with Virginians. They were on alert.

Outside Williamsburg, a company of Virginia militia, under the command of Patrick Henry, set up camp on May 3. Henry's men remained there for several days while negotiators tried to reach a settlement about the gunpowder. Fearing for his life, Dunmore warned the colonists that, if he were attacked, he would "declare Freedom to the Slaves, and reduce the City of *Williamsburg* to Ashes." Finally, a friend of Dunmore agreed to pay the colonists £330 for the gunpowder, and the militia left.

The Boys' Company

Less than two months after Dunmore's men broke into the Magazine, a few Williamsburg boys did, too. The boys, who were excited about all the political and military goings-on, were part of a group that called themselves the Boys' Company. Their captain was only fourteen years old. There's no record of the Boys' Company ever fighting in a battle as a unit, but some members later joined the Continental army.

When the boys went inside, they discovered that the Magazine had been booby-trapped. A spring triggered a shotgun, injuring three boys. Many in Williamsburg blamed Dunmore, and a few days later he fled the city, taking refuge in a British ship anchored at nearby Yorktown.

Wise to the Words

🥁 A *magazine* is where military equipment, including guns and ammunition, is stored. The magazine you get in the mail or at a newsstand is where a lot of information is stored.

🥁 A *militia* is a group of civilians trained as soldiers but not part of a regular paid army.

🥁 *Redcoats* were British soldiers.

George Wythe House

George Wythe ranks among colonial America's finest lawyers, legal scholars, and teachers. In 1779, Wythe joined the College of William and Mary faculty as the first law professor in the British colonies.

Perhaps the most handsome house in Williamsburg, the two-story brick residence of George Wythe is believed to have been designed in the mid-1750s by Wythe's father-in-law, the surveyor, builder, and planter Richard Taliaferro. Taliaferro built the supper room in the Governor's Palace at about the same time.

While preparing for the siege of Yorktown, during the Revolutionary War, George Washington used the Wythe House as his headquarters.

Outbuildings on the property include a smokehouse, a kitchen, a laundry, a poultry house, a lumber house, a well, a dovecote, two privies, and a stable.

A Famous Teacher

George Wythe left his mark in many ways, but maybe most of all as a teacher. Among his students was Thomas Jefferson, who became president of the United States. Wythe wasn't in Philadelphia when the Declaration of Independence was ready for signing, but, out of respect for Wythe, Virginia's signers of the Declaration left room for his signature at the top of their group of signatures.

Wise to the Words

🥁 *Wythe* is pronounced "With."

🥁 A *dovecote* is a pigeon coop.

🥁 A *privy* is an eighteenth-century bathroom.

🥁 *Taliaferro* is pronounced "Tolliver."

Wheelwright

Given that almost everybody needed carts and thousands were in use, wheelwrights were as vital in their time as auto mechanics are today. They cut, shaped, and joined wood to make wheels that stood up to rough roads and rougher fields. Hubs, spokes, and rim were wood. An iron, not rubber, tire usually circled the outside of the rim. Cart wheels were "dished," or bowed out, from the cart to reduce the strain on the wheels caused by the swaying walk of animals like oxen.

Wheelwrights do not make just wheels. They construct many kinds of eighteenth-century wheeled vehicles, including carts, wagons, and riding chairs.

Wise to the Words

🪣 A *riding chair* is a two-wheeled vehicle with a seat for the driver and, sometimes, a passenger. It was very fashionable in the colonies.

🪣 Don't know what a *spoke-shave* is? Ask a tradesperson to show you one. (HINT: It has to do with both shaving and the spokes of a wheel.)

Basketmaker

Most Virginians in the eighteenth-century lived in the country on small farms, and these families made their own baskets. Both boys and girls learned to make baskets at an early age, first learning to weave and, as they grew older, helping to split apart white oak trees for material. Because Virginians either made their own baskets or imported them, no one in the colony actually earned a living as a basketmaker, but you can see baskets being made in an outbuilding on the George Wythe property.

Governor's Palace

At the end of Palace Green stands the Governor's Palace, symbol of the king's authority. The Palace was home to seven British governors, the last being John Murray, Earl of Dunmore. When the colonies gained their independence, the Palace became the residence of the first two governors of an independent Virginia, Patrick Henry and Thomas Jefferson.

The Governor's Palace was completed in 1722. About twenty-five servants and slaves, including stewards, personal servants, butlers, footmen, cooks, laundresses, gardeners, maids, grooms, and laborers, were needed to keep the Palace open and functioning.

When the capital of the commonwealth of Virginia moved to Richmond, the Palace was used for a short time as headquarters by General Charles Lee of the Continental army. After the Battle of Yorktown, the last decisive battle of the American Revolution, it became a hospital for soldiers wounded in the battle. While in use for that purpose, the original building was destroyed by fire on December 22, 1781. Despite the occupancy of over one hundred sick and wounded soldiers, only one person died.

The reconstruction you see today was completed in 1934. You won't want—or be able—to miss the impressive display of muskets and swords on the walls of the front entrance hall. The weapons were meant to impress colonists with the governor's power. Another fun place to visit at the Palace is the maze in the back of the garden. Many large estates in England had mazes to entertain guests when they came to visit. They were definitely not just for children! Also, be sure not to miss the Palace kitchen.

Colonials didn't have central heating, but they did have fireplaces.

Imagine what it must have been like to live in the Palace, as did the children of Lord Dunmore, the last royal governor of Virginia. Six of his children moved to Williamsburg with their mother in 1774. (Lord Dunmore was already here.) Another child, named Virginia, was born in the Palace in December 1774. The children were surrounded by symbols of the power and authority of the king of England. See if you can find some of those symbols. Here are some clues: look at the front gate, the top of the cupola, the back door, and the bathhouse.

Party Like It's 1771

When the cream of Williamsburg society got together, it was often at the Palace. In October 1771, the *Virginia Gazette* reported, "On Friday evening his Excellency the Governor gave a ball at the palace, in honour of our gracious Sovereign, it being the anniversary of his accession to the throne. The company was numerous and brilliant, and the entertainment elegant."

Everything Including the Kitchen Sink

When the royal governor Lord Botetourt died in 1770, a full list of his possessions was written down. Over 16,500 items were listed as being stored in and around the Palace. The contents of a single Palace storeroom included jars of raisins, coffee from Turkey and India, Congo tea and spices, slave shoes, egg strainers, balls of pack thread, white macaroons, ginseng and snakeroot, soap and hair powder, paintbrushes, carpet brooms, hearth brooms, cane brooms, cane whisks, hair-dust brushes, bottle brushes, plate brushes, clothes brushes, shoe brushes, flat clamp brushes, and mops.

Colonials didn't have matches, but they did have flint and steel.

Palace Kitchen

What did the royal governors like Lord Dunmore like to eat for dinner? At the Palace kitchen, you can see which of the dishes on the table you would like to eat. You can also see the cooks at work preparing these foods using the equipment and recipes of the eighteenth century. Sometimes you can even see the colonial way of making chocolate.

Colonials didn't have chocolate candy bars, but they did have hot chocolate to drink.

Cooks roasted meat over hot coals using a spit and a clock jack. The meat is put on a metal bar called a *spit*. The clock jack turns the spit to keep the meat cooking evenly—and to keep it from burning on one side! Winding the clock jack would be a job for kids in the kitchen. How often you have to wind the clock jack depends on various factors. You might have to wind it every two minutes or it might run for as long as twenty minutes before it needs winding again.

Colonials didn't have ovens or stovetops, but they did have fireplaces.

You may also want to visit the icehouse to see where the ice for making ice cream was stored and the back pantry to see the molds and equipment used for making the ice cream into fancy shapes. By the way, if you hate waiting for dessert, you would have loved eating with the governor. Heavy sweets like cakes and pies were served with the meats and vegetables all through the meal.

In colonial times, both boys and girls were expected to help cook. Younger kids washed dishes and brought in wood and water from the well, and older ones learned about plucking chickens, scaling fish, and the basics of cooking.

Jefferson's Drawings

Not only did Thomas Jefferson write the Declaration of Independence and become president of the United States, he was also an architect. In 1779, while he was governor and lived in the Palace, Jefferson drew a plan of the building, maybe because he was planning to remodel it. Two years later, the Palace burned down. In the 1930s, when Colonial Williamsburg rebuilt the Palace, Jefferson's drawings helped architects know what it looked like.

Wise to the Word

🎲 *Botetourt* is pronounced "BOT-a-tot."

Public Hospital

Warning!

Some parts of this exhibit may be disturbing. Ask your parents whether they think it's okay for you to go.

The Public Hospital for Persons of Insane and Disordered Minds was the first institution in North America devoted solely to the treatment of people with mental health disorders. The first patient was admitted on October 12, 1773.

The Public Hospital was founded at the urging of Governor Francis Fauquier. Fauquier was worried about that "poor unhappy set of People who are deprived of their Senses and wander about the Country, terrifying the Rest of their Fellow Creatures." The Public Hospital was designed to serve dangerous individuals as well as patients who might be treated and discharged.

Before then, if people with mental health disorders weren't cared for at home, they were often put in the jail. At first, the hospital wasn't much better than a jail. The building housed twenty-four cells. Each cell had a heavy door with a barred window, a mattress, a chamber pot, and an iron ring in the wall to which a patient's wrist or leg chains could be attached.

According to the theories of the day, mental illness was a disease of the brain and nervous system, and people with mental illness *chose* to be irrational. Treatment included drugs, restraint, cold baths, bloodletting, and blistering ointments. Amazingly, about 20 percent of inmates were discharged as "cured."

Today, the Public Hospital contains an exhibit showing changes in psychiatric care from 1773 to 1885, when the original structure burned down. You can see that care became more kindly as time went on.

Wise to the Words

- *Fauquier* is pronounced "FAW-keer."
- A *chamber pot* was a pot that served as a toilet.

DeWitt Wallace Decorative Arts Museum

The DeWitt Wallace Decorative Arts Museum houses a large collection of American and British furniture, metals, ceramics, glass, paintings, prints, firearms, and textiles from the seventeenth, eighteenth, and nineteenth centuries. Enter the museum through the front door of the Public Hospital.

Two Georges

Be sure to see the portrait of George Washington by Charles Willson Peale. Who is our first president looking at? Can you find a patriotic symbol in the painting? Look in the background and decide who won the battle. Now compare the painting to that of George II just around the corner. George II was the grandfather of George III, who was king of England during the American Revolution. What is the same about these paintings? What is different?

A Tea Party

Can you find the "No Stamp Act" teapot? What better way to show your support for the patriot cause than over a cup of tea.

Abby Aldrich Rockefeller Folk Art Museum

The Abby Aldrich Rockefeller Folk Art Museum offers exhibitions of American folk art. Folk artists and craftspeople work outside the mainstream of art to record aspects of everyday life. Bold colors, simplified shapes, and imaginative surface patterns can be seen in the variety of paintings, carvings, toys, weather vanes, and needlework.

Be sure to see the exhibit called Down on the Farm. You can see folk art from the nineteenth and twentieth centuries and enjoy a story about a great little dog named Prince. This exhibit is a great place to relax and enjoy creating a bit of something yourself. You can even put some of your own artwork on exhibit.

Wise to the Word

A *weather vane* shows you the direction the wind is blowing.

Family guides are available to pick up and enjoy while visiting the Art Museums of Colonial Williamsburg. You can also check out Teen Takes, an audio guide developed by teenagers. Check ahead for family programs in the education studio.

Shopping and Eating

Within the Historic Area there are plenty of places to shop and eat. You can find great colonial toys, like marbles and Aesop's fables playing cards and bilbo catchers, and you can try some colonial specialties at the taverns and bakery.

Wise to the Word

A *bilbo catcher* is a ball and stick game in which you have to catch the ball with the stick. It came from Bilboa, Spain.

Places to Shop

Mary Dickinson Store

Look your eighteenth-century best in handmade petticoats, short gowns, cloaks, mitts, caps, and straw hats. Also toiletries and jewelry.

John Greenhow Store

Tools, home accessories, toys, and other goods similar to those sold by Mr. Greenhow in the eighteenth century.

Colonials didn't have paper bags, but they did have baskets.

The Golden Ball

Rings, earrings, pendants, and charms in sterling silver and 14-karat gold, including items handmade by Colonial Williamsburg's silversmiths.

Market House

An open-air market selling toys, hats, pottery, and baskets. You can also rent eighteenth-century costumes for boys and girls here. Weather permitting.

Post Office

Reproduction prints, maps, books, stationery, quill pens, ink and inkwells, and sealing wax. Postcards and stamps are also available, and, if you mail items from here, they will be hand-cancelled with an eighteenth-century postmark.

Prentis Store

Handcrafted items made by Colonial Williamsburg tradespeople.

Tarpley, Thompson & Company

Tavern ware, pewter, and glassware from the historic dining taverns.

William Pitt Store

Toys, games, children's period clothing, hats, and jewelry. Colonials didn't have chewing gum, but they did have rock candy.

Places to Eat

Christiana Campbell's Tavern

Christiana Campbell opened her tavern in 1771. A distinguished clientele, including George Washington, patronized her business.

Christiana Campbell's Tavern specializes in seafood.

Chowning's Tavern

Josiah Chowning opened his tavern in 1766. The menu today is light food such as soups and sandwiches. Legend has it that sandwiches were introduced in the eighteenth century and named after the Earl of Sandwich. Colonials didn't have potato chips, but they did have popcorn.

In the early evening, interpreters sometimes lead guests in sing-alongs while other costumed entertainers play games, do magic tricks, and tell jokes. (After 8 p.m., the entertainment gets a bit racier!)

King's Arms Tavern

For more than thirty years, Jane Vobe operated the original King's Arms Tavern. She was one of several female tavern keepers in town. At some point during the Revolution, her tavern was renamed "The Eagle."

The King's Arms offers a chophouse menu featuring prime rib, pork chops, and game pye.

61

Shields Tavern

James Shields took over the tavern in the early 1740s. Today the tavern serves home-style food, including lunch favorites like hot dogs and hamburgers.

Colonials didn't have mayonnaise, but they did have ketchup and mustard.

Huzzah! BBQ Grille

A family-friendly restaurant located near the Visitor Center, Huzzah! offers barbecued chicken, pork, and beef as well as pizza and other everyday favorites.

Raleigh Tavern Bakery

Cookies, cakes, and breads freshly baked in eighteenth-century style as well as soups and sandwiches. Hot and cold beverages including root beer and apple cider.

Colonials didn't have soda, but they did have apple cider.

To learn more about Colonial Williamsburg and for lots of fun games and activities, go to colonialwilliamsburg.org/kids

Index

This book was made possible by the generous support of the Steven and Sheila Miller Foundation of Houston, Texas.